D1257294

CANADA

Star of the North

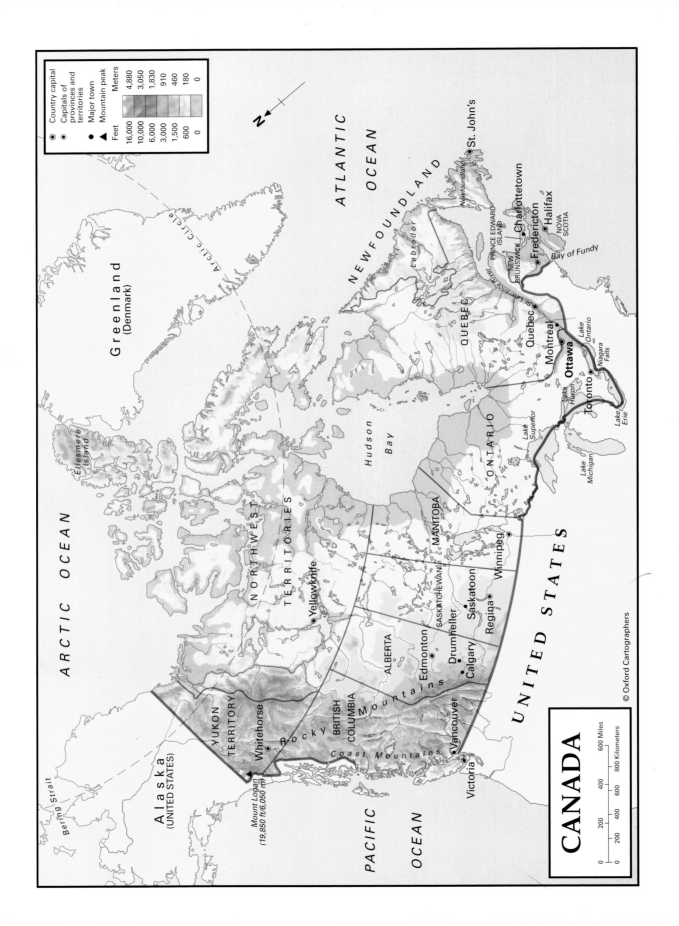

CANADA

ARCTIC OCEAN

ATLANTIC OCEAN

PACIFIC OCEAN

Greenland (Denmark)

Ellesmere Island

Arctic Circle

Bering Strait

Alaska (UNITED STATES)

Mount Logan (19,850 ft/6,050 m)

YUKON TERRITORY

NORTHWEST TERRITORIES

Whitehorse

Yellowknife

BRITISH COLUMBIA

Rocky Mountains

Coast Mountains

Victoria

Vancouver

ALBERTA

Edmonton

Drumheller

Calgary

SASKATCHEWAN

Saskatoon

Regina

MANITOBA

Winnipeg

Hudson Bay

Labrador

NEWFOUNDLAND

Newfoundland

St. John's

ONTARIO

QUEBEC

Lake Superior

Lake Michigan

Lake Huron

Lake Erie

Lake Ontario

Niagara Falls

Toronto

Ottawa

Montreal

Quebec

St. Lawrence River

PRINCE EDWARD ISLAND

Charlottetown

NEW BRUNSWICK

Fredericton

NOVA SCOTIA

Halifax

Bay of Fundy

UNITED STATES

© Oxford Cartographers

Legend
- ✳ Country capital
- ⊙ Capitals of provinces and territories
- ● Major town
- ▲ Mountain peak

Feet	Meters
16,000	4,880
10,000	3,050
6,000	1,830
3,000	910
1,500	460
600	180
0	0

600 Miles
800 Kilometers
400
600
200
400
200
0
0

CANADA

Star of the North

Shelley Swanson Sateren

BENCHMARK BOOKS

MARSHALL CAVENDISH

NEW YORK

With thanks to Consul Paul Bennett at the Canadian Consulate General in Minneapolis, Minnesota, for his expert reading of this manuscript

Many thanks to Gerry Foley, Public Affairs Officer of the Canadian Consulate General in Minneapolis, Minnesota, for his tremendous help in researching this book. Special thanks also to Jennifer Stromberg and her family in Saskatchewan and to Dr. Bill Beahen, Force Historian of the Royal Canadian Mounted Police, for providing me with information.

Benchmark Books
Marshall Cavendish Corporation
99 White Plains Road
Tarrytown, New York 10591-9001

© Marshall Cavendish Corporation 1996

Library of Congress Cataloging-in-Publication Data
Sateren, Shelley Swanson.
    Canada : star of the north / Shelley Swanson Sateren.
        p.   cm. — (Exploring cultures of the world)
    Includes bibliographical references.
    Summary: Describes the geography, history, people, and culture of the second largest country in the world.
    ISBN 0-7614-0199-7
    1. Canada—Juvenile literature.   [1. Canada.]   I. Title. II. Series.
F1008.2.S28   1996
971—dc20   95-25703

Printed and bound in the U.S.A.

Book design by Carol Matsuyama
Photo research by Sandy Jones

Front cover: Folk dancing
Back cover: Harp seal pup, Gulf of St. Lawrence

Photo Credits

Front cover: courtesy of Ellefsen/FPG International; back cover and page 9: courtesy of Jeff Foott Photography; pages 3, 28, 38: Fred McKinney/FPG International; page 6: Courtesy Royal Canadian Mounted Police Archives; pages 10, 36: Thomas Kitchin/Tom Stack & Associates; page 12: R. Garnett/Visual Contact; page 15: Bridgeman/Art Resource, NY; pages 18, 25: Photo, John Elk III; page 22: Chris Mooney/FPG International; pages 23, 33: Purcell/WORDS & PICTURES/Carl Purcell; pages 27, 46: Robin Karpin Photo; pages 31, 54: Photo, Wolfgang Kaehler; page 35: Jurgen Vogt/Image Bank; page 41: Esbin-Anderson/Omni-Photo Communications; page 42: R. Redshaw/Visual Contact; page 43: The Bettmann Archives; page 44: REUTERS/Mal Langsolon/ARCHIVE PHOTO; page 45: FOTOPIC/Omni-Photo Communications; page 48: Photo, Robert Fried; page 51: Photo, Jim West; page 52: Kirkendall-Spring/Boreland Stock Photo; page 56: Photo, Rubin Klass

Contents

This 1870s photograph shows Jerry Potts (the man standing on the right with dark hair and a long mustache) *with several Mounties and two Indian men.*

1

GEOGRAPHY AND HISTORY

A King-Size Country

Without a Map or Compass

On a bitterly cold winter night in 1874, a small, mustached man wearing fringed buckskins climbed onto his horse. He rode across the snow-covered Canadian prairie, leading ten Mounties, members of the recently created Royal Canadian Mounted Police (RCMP), on horseback. They headed toward an illegal whiskey traders' camp miles away.

The Mounties arrested the whiskey traders, then set off, back through the fierce winds and blinding snow of a full-scale blizzard. The snowfall was so thick the travelers could see no farther than the throw of a snowball. They were in great danger of getting lost and freezing to death.

Their guide had neither map nor compass. He relied solely on his keen sense of direction to lead the Mounties safely to shelter.

This scout, known as the best guide in Canada's Wild West, was Jerry Potts. A Métis (may-TEE) Indian, Potts was famous for his frontier skills and immense bravery. Because of his vast knowledge of the prairie, the Mounties found shelter and food and water in the wild. Jerry Potts served as the RCMP's guide for twenty-two years.

Potts's skills helped bring law to the Canadian West. He also spoke several Indian languages and served as a peacemaker between the Mounties and the Indians.

Nature Rules

Canada is a king-size country, the second largest in the world. Only Russia is larger. Almost completely surrounded by oceans—the Arctic, the Atlantic, and the Pacific—Canada has the longest coastline of any country. If its 150,000-mile (241,350-kilometer) coast were stretched into a straight line, it would circle the world six times!

Canadian winters are *cold*. Every year about one hundred Canadians lose their lives as a result of the extreme cold. A farmer walking from his house to his barn during a blinding blizzard can lose his way and even his life in the freezing snowdrifts of a Canadian winter.

For thousands of years, nature has ruled in this land. Canada's awesome size and harsh winters created great challenges for its first peoples and its later settlers. Much of this enormous country remains wilderness even today. Wild animals roam undisturbed in Canada's hundreds upon thousands of miles of tundra, mountains, and glaciers.

Ten Provinces and Two Territories

Canada is divided into ten provinces and two territories. Some of them share similar geographic features.

The Atlantic Provinces

The four small provinces on Canada's Atlantic Coast are known as the Atlantic Provinces—Newfoundland, Nova Scotia, New Brunswick, and Prince Edward Island.

A winter storm clears off the mountaintops in Alberta's Jasper National Park. The dangerously low winter temperatures in Canada's wilderness can claim lives if hikers or skiers are careless.

Between November and June in Newfoundland, the strait that separates the mainland area of the province—which is also called Labrador—from the island of Newfoundland is completely filled with ice. When the long winter ends, huge icebergs float in the sea and can bring disaster to ships and ferries. It was off the coast of Newfoundland that the *Titanic* struck an iceberg and sank many years ago.

Nova Scotia, shaped like a whale swimming southwest, juts into the Atlantic Ocean. It is almost completely surrounded by the sea, except for a narrow strip of land that joins it to the rest of Canada. This is a land of sand and surf and rocky cliffs that plunge into the ocean.

In New Brunswick's Bay of Fundy, the tides are as high as a four-story building! Twice each day, one hundred billion tons of water swirl up the bay's shores and back down again. Over the years, these tides have sculpted the rocky coast into

Nova Scotia's pretty seaside villages, brightly painted fishing boats, and rugged coastline draw thousands of tourists each year.

curious shapes. Many of the rocks look like giant flowerpots.

Prince Edward Island is Canada's smallest province. It makes up just 1 percent of Canada's land. No place on Prince Edward Island is farther than ten miles (sixteen kilometers) from the ocean. All around the island are lighthouses that protect boats and ships from the dangerous reefs and sandbars.

Canada's South

Canada's two largest provinces—Ontario and Quebec—are also the country's southernmost provinces. Canada's most southern tip is in Ontario, on Lake Erie. This point is so far south that it's in line with northern California.

Ontario is Canada's second-largest province. It is home to Ottawa, Canada's capital, and to one-third of the nation's people. Niagara Falls, one of the world's seven natural wonders, is found there, too.

Much of Canada's land is made up of the Canadian Shield—giant fields of huge rock that formed six hundred million years ago. The forests and mineral-rich lands of the Canadian Shield make up Ontario's north.

Quebec is Canada's largest province, covering nearly one-sixth of the whole country. Quebec is more than twice the size of Texas and three times bigger than France. The mighty St. Lawrence River is Quebec's most important feature. The river divides Canada from the United States and connects the Great Lakes with the Atlantic Ocean. Whales are a common sight at the mouth of the St. Lawrence.

The Prairie Provinces

West of Ontario lie Canada's three Prairie Provinces—Manitoba, Saskatchewan, and Alberta.

Farmland blankets southern Manitoba with endless fields of wheat and sunflowers. In the northern town of Churchill, on Hudson Bay, the people are careful before going outdoors in the spring. They must first check to make sure the streets are clear of their springtime visitors—polar bears.

Saskatchewan is Canada's greatest producer of wheat. Gigantic grain farms are common on the Wheat Province's flat land, which stretches as far as the eye can see. In the south lie the dry, desertlike badlands. A *Tyrannosaurus rex* skeleton was uncovered in Saskatchewan's badlands in

Southern Alberta is home to huge farms and endless fields of cropland, just like the other two Prairie Provinces.

1994, one of only about a dozen that have ever been found.

Albertans are lucky. They live in the sunniest province. Alberta is also home to beautiful forests and the breathtaking Rocky Mountains. In the south Alberta shares the badlands with Saskatchewan. In this dry expanse, water and wind have created strange shapes in the sandstone. Years ago the Plains Indians named these tall columns with caps on top hoodoos. They believed hoodoos were petrified stone giants that came alive at night and threw stones at people.

The Pacific Coast

The province of British Columbia, on Canada's Pacific Coast, is rich in natural beauty and natural resources. Animals that have disappeared from much of the rest of Canada, such as grizzly bears, eagles, and cougars, still roam through this westernmost province.

Thanks to warm, moist Pacific Ocean airstreams, southern British Columbia enjoys milder weather than the rest of Canada. Heavy rainfall between the Pacific Ocean and the steep Coast Mountains has created rain forests, in which six-hundred-year-old Douglas fir trees still stand today.

The Far North

Arctic winters in Canada's two territories—the Yukon and the Northwest Territories—are bitterly cold. In Canada's far north temperatures fall as low as -75°F (-59°C).

Frostbite can strike in seconds on an arctic winter day, and just one mistake outdoors can cost a human life. There are only a few weeks in the year when temperatures in the far north rise above freezing. Sometimes it even snows during the Arctic's warmest month of the year—July! One-half of Canada's land is permafrost, ground that stays frozen year-round.

Canada's lowest temperature, -81°F (-63°C), was recorded during a Yukon winter. Few people choose to live in this cold territory in which people outnumber grizzly bears only four to one.

The Northwest Territories is really just one huge territory (although by 1999 it will become two, when the Inuit territory of Nunavut is born). One-third of Canada's land, the Northwest Territories is so large that travelers must spend two days on airplanes to fly completely across it. Canada's northernmost point of land, on Ellesmere Island in the Northwest Territories, is only about 500 miles (805 kilometers) from the North Pole.

The few Canadians who live on the shores of the Arctic Ocean hear haunting, groaning sounds as giant plates of ice in the ocean shift and grind together. Those who live in the far north also experience very sunny summers. Canada's Arctic is

A BRAND-NEW TERRITORY

In 1999 the Northwest Territories will be divided into two separate territories. The eastern half will be populated mainly by the Inuit people. This new territory will be called Nunavut (NUN-uh-vuht).

The Inuit asked the Canadian government for the rights to own and manage this land, and they received them. They will take charge of Nunavut's government and the land, which they have always believed to be theirs. Nunavut means "our land" in the Inuit language. Inuit leaders have begun to educate and train their people, preparing them to take over government jobs.

The creation of Nunavut is a dream come true for these native people. They will own more land and shares of natural resources—worth many millions of dollars. The Inuit who live in Nunavut will be equal partners in Canada. This territory is also the largest land claim in Canadian history.

the "land of the midnight sun." In midsummer, in the northernmost regions of the Northwest Territories, the sun shines all night long for about four weeks. In midwinter there the sun doesn't rise for about four weeks and the days remain dark. Farther south at the timberline, people experience about two weeks of complete midsummer lightness and two weeks of complete midwinter darkness.

The First Canadians

About 35,000 years ago, humans began to wander across the Bering Strait from Asia to Alaska. These first people ever to set foot on the continent of North America were later called Indians. Some of them became nomads—following wild herds of animals around North America and hunting them for food—while others became farmers or fishermen.

About 5,000 years ago, another group of people crossed the Bering Strait. They traveled to the far north in the Arctic and remained there. They hunted seal and walrus in the Arctic Ocean, traveling in their own invention—the kayak. Although these people are often called Eskimos, today they call themselves the Inuit (IN-oo-it; IN-yoo-it), which means "the people."

For thousands of years, the Inuit and the Indians lived without knowledge of the rest of the world. Yet they developed detailed systems of government. They invented clever tools for hunting and defending themselves. They worked with the land and sea so that most of the native people thrived. But all this started to change in the 1500s, when Europeans began to arrive in their ships.

Fortunes in Fish and Fur

One day in the 1530s, the French explorer Jacques Cartier stepped off his boat and onto the shore of a northern land. As the story goes, he asked a group of natives where he was, and they replied, *Kanata*. This word meant "settlement" in their language. Cartier returned to France and told the people all about this marvelous land called Canada.

France and England sent several explorers overseas in the 1500s and 1600s to search for a route to China—and Cartier was one of them. The explorers never discovered the route, but they found something else of great worth: a land rich in fish and fur.

The explorers' find launched a busy fur trade in Canada. Beaver

An early map of Canada drawn in the 1530s by a French explorer. The man in the long red coat (standing in the center of the map among his followers) is Jacques Cartier.

15

pelts brought high prices in Europe where they were made into high-fashion hats.

Fur companies hired young men to search the wilderness for fur-trading Indians. These men, called voyageurs (voi-uh-ZHAR), "travelers" in French, were strong men who often wore red wool caps and deerskin leggings. Voyageurs paddled their canoes for sixteen to eighteen hours each day. They carried supply packs that weighed as much as ninety pounds (forty-one kilograms). The voyageurs' job was hard and dangerous, and these men often met with an early death from disease or drowning in the wilderness.

The fur trade also made great problems for the Indians' centuries-old culture. When the native people began to hunt animals to earn money, they no longer used their creative skills to make the things they needed. Many Indians also caught diseases from the white traders and settlers. Thousands of native people died.

The fur trade lasted for two hundred years. It was so important in the settlement and creation of Canada that the beaver remains one of the nation's symbols today along with the maple leaf, moose, and schooner—a multimasted sailing ship. The beaver is Ontario's provincial symbol. As a national symbol, the beaver appears on the Canadian nickel.

A Country Is Born

In the 1700s France and England began to fight over the right to own this rich northern land. France lost fort after fort to England, and finally in 1759, England conquered. Britain now ruled the northern colonies that would one day become the country of Canada.

Years passed, and the United States to the south became

CANADIAN GOVERNMENT

Canada is a parliamentary democracy. Her Majesty Queen Elizabeth II of Great Britain is queen of Canada and head of state, but her role is symbolic.

Canada's leader is the prime minister, who is the leader of the party with the most number of seats in the House of Commons. The prime minister chooses a cabinet to help run the government. There are about forty ministers in the cabinet. Each minister runs one or several departments, such as foreign affairs and international trade, natural resources, defense, or health.

Canada's national parliament is divided into two houses—the Senate with 104 members appointed by the governor general on the recommendation of the prime minister—and the House of Commons with 295 members elected by popular vote. The House of Commons is much more powerful than the Senate and all bills have their beginnings there.

more powerful. The northern colonies realized they had to protect their lands. They united and created the Dominion of Canada on July 1, 1867, Canada's birthday. The new country was granted limited self-rule, with its own government. But it still belonged to the British Empire, and the queen of England remained its monarch.

In the 1870s and 1880s the building of a cross-country railroad brought many new immigrants to Canada, mainly from Ireland and China. They took jobs laying thousands of miles of railroad track, blasting through granite in the Rocky Mountains and building tunnels. In the early 1900s wheat replaced fur as Canada's top resource. Many Canadian wheat farmers profited, and thousands more immigrants arrived from continental Europe and the United States to join them.

Since the 1930s Canada has been almost entirely free from Britain. In 1982, when Canada was given the right to change, or amend, its own constitution, the last tie to its former European ruler was cut. Today Canada remains completely in charge of its policies—both at home and abroad.

A town crier at a historic site in Halifax, Nova Scotia, carries on the centuries-old tradition of making public announcements by shouting them in the streets.

2
THE PEOPLE

Canadians Today

Canada is a nation of immigrants. The native people—the Indians and the Inuit—represent only 2 percent of Canadians today. All other Canadians or their ancestors came to this northern land by ship or car or airplane from somewhere else. The French and the English have been the main immigrants to Canada since the 1600s. But today there are more than seventy cultural groups in the country.

Many Tongues

More than sixty languages are spoken in Canada. The country has two official languages: English and French. Throughout the country, road signs appear in both languages. The information on all products in stores must be printed in French and English. Government workers must speak both of these languages, and almost 16 percent of Canada's population is bilingual as well.

Most of the people in Quebec are French-Canadian. Eighty-five percent of them speak French as their first language. Quebec has the greatest number of French immigrants in North America.

THE QUEBEC QUESTION

In Quebec some of the people want their province to separate from Canada and become its own country—a French-speaking nation.

In the 1960s a number of French-speaking people in Quebec began to voice their desire to separate from Canada. The province held a vote in 1980 to answer this question. Nearly 60 percent of Quebec's people voted against leaving Canada.

In the 1990s the new party in charge of Quebec's government, the Parti Québécois (kay-beh-KWAH), promised another vote. If more than 50 percent of the people were to vote to make the province of Quebec a separate country, Quebec would begin to work toward that goal.

Quebec held this historic vote on October 30, 1995, and more than four and a half million of the province's people voted. The result was 50.5 percent to 49.5 percent, with those wanting an independent country of Quebec losing by only 1 percent of the vote. But they say they will soon try again for independence.

Some Québécois want their province to be a separate sovereignty. It is not always clear what these words mean. They usually involve greater international recognition, control over social programs, and the promotion of their culture and language.

Many Faiths

The law in Canada gives people the freedom to practice any religion they choose. Most Canadians have chosen Christianity. Centuries ago Canada's French immigrants were Roman Catholics. Today more than eleven million Canadians are Roman Catholic, most of them French speaking.

Smaller numbers of Canadians practice other religions, such as Judaism, the Sikh religion from India, Islam, Buddhism, and Hinduism.

Most native peoples in Canada have become Christians, although some still practice their traditional religions, worshiping the Great Spirit who created the universe. In the far north, Christian Inuit families gather to worship at St. Jude's

Cathedral in Iqaluit (ee-ha-loo-eat), the Northwest Territories, in a white, dome-shaped wooden church that looks like an igloo.

City and Country Life

There simply aren't that many people in this huge country—about twenty-nine million. Though Canada is the second-largest country in the world, it ranks thirty-first in population. The United States has a population ten times larger than that of Canada, though the United States is 10 percent smaller in size. Fewer people live in the whole country of Canada than live in the state of California! But Canada's population is growing at a faster rate today than any other country in the Western world.

Half of Canada's people live close to the Great Lakes and along the St. Lawrence River—near Toronto and Montreal—because of the warmer climate, good farmland, and business centers found there. Compared to the rest of Canada, which is mostly rural or unpopulated, the far south seems bustling and crowded. Shuping, a girl who lives in Toronto's Chinatown, must be very careful when crossing the city's busy streets. It hardly seems possible that in Shuping's same province, in northern Ontario, a person could walk down a road through the woods and not meet a car for miles.

Most Canadians live in urban areas, yet the nation has only a few large cities. Toronto, Ontario, is the largest, with about three-and-a-half million people. The second largest, Montreal, Quebec, is a city built on an island that is actually an extinct volcano. The third-largest city in Canada is Vancouver, in the province of British Columbia, on the Pacific Ocean. Vancouver is Canada's busiest port city.

Ottawa, the capital of Canada, is small in size but large in importance. The government buildings of the nation's capital overlook the Rideau Canal, which freezes over in the wintertime, allowing some government workers to ice-skate to work.

Canadian cities have less crime than cities in the neighboring United States. Unlike in America where many private citizens own guns, in Canada gun permits are harder to get. The Royal Canadian Mounted Police—Canada's national police force—rarely uses guns. Throughout its history the RCMP has always worked to settle differences peacefully. Today the Mountie in his red uniform is a symbol of the Canadians' strong desire for law and order.

Canadian Mounties on parade at Expo 1986 in Vancouver

Citizens of Ottawa enjoy ice-skating and strolling on the frozen Rideau Canal in the wintertime.

For Most, A Comfortable Life

Most Canadians are middle class and enjoy a good quality of life. They have enough money to live comfortably and plenty of food to eat.

Canada doesn't have as many poor and homeless people

as the United States does, and the gap between the "haves" and the "have nots" is narrower than in the United States. This is partly because of Canada's social programs, such as free medical care. Every Canadian may be checked by a doctor without being charged a penny. But Canadians also pay high taxes to help pay for these social programs. Today the national and provincial governments are looking at ways to save money, so some of these programs may be cut back.

Where Canadians live often determines what jobs they have and how much money they are able to earn. People fish for a living on the coast. They farm on the prairie. They work in mining jobs up north. Many others across the country have jobs in the forest, manufacturing, and service industries.

The Atlantic Provinces are suffering today, in part because the fishing industry there isn't earning much money anymore. Ocean waters have been overfished. The Canadian government gives money to the Atlantic Provinces to help them through their hard times. Many Canadians believe that the richer provinces should help the poorer ones so that as many Canadians as possible may live comfortably.

For many years, two other groups of Canadians have not enjoyed the good quality of life that most Canadians do. These are the Indians and the Inuit. In the 1800s and 1900s, when immigrants flooded into Canada, the Indians lost their lands and hunting grounds. White settlers introduced them to alcohol and guns, which created problems for the Indians. The Inuit experienced similar troubles in the north. The native people grew poorer while many immigrants became rich.

The native people remain among the poorest of Canadian citizens. About half of the Indian population live on reservations, some of which have poor water quality and too few good

These Canadians from Digby Harbor, Nova Scotia, make their living by fishing for scallops.

jobs available to the people. More than half of Canada's Indian and Inuit children live in poverty today. Canada's native people, or First Nations, are, though, receiving land claim settlements that give them greater control over resources such as lumber as well as the power to govern themselves.

One Canada or Twelve?

A rainbow of colorful cultures exists in Canada, with immigrants from many countries offering their unique traditions. In Victoria, British Columbia, people still serve English tea every day. Every summer the hills of Nova Scotia echo with the sound of bagpipes played by Scottish Canadians. And French-speaking Acadians—descendants of immigrants who settled in the Acadian Peninsula of New Brunswick centuries ago—still bake bread every day and play the fiddle in the French tradition.

Since World War II most immigrants have settled in large

SAY IT IN FRENCH

Here is how you would say some common words and phrases in French.

Hello or good morning:	*Bonjour* (bohn-ZHOOR)
How are you?:	*Comment allez-vous?* (KUH-mahn ta-lay-VOO)
Very well, thank you:	*Très bien, merci* (treh B'YEN, mehr-SEE)
Good-bye:	*Au revoir* (o-RVWAR)
What is it?:	*Qu'est-ce que c'est?* (KESS-kuh-SAY)

SAY IT IN CANADIAN ENGLISH

Canadian English is different in many ways from the English spoken in the United States. Some pronunciations and word meanings are different.

been: pronounced bean
again: pronounced ah-GAIN
hydro: means electricity

constable: means policeman
tap: means faucet

A common expression in Canadian English is the word *eh.* It is pronounced as a long "a" and is tacked onto the end of many sentences, such as, "I'm going for a walk, eh?"

cities. People from many different countries mingle in Vancouver, Calgary, Toronto, and Montreal. Others live in smaller towns and throughout Canada's vast countryside.

Immigrant groups tend to practice the traditions they have brought with them from their homelands. One reason for this is that Canada encourages the celebration of many different cultures. Another reason is geography. Huge distances separate Canadian towns. Mountains, enormous lakes, and seemingly endless prairie separate people. Groups have often remained separate, and so they have kept their traditions alive.

These ranchers who live on the Canadian prairie have very different concerns from the Canadians who live in big cities, on the coasts, or in the far north.

These great distances between communities of people can make Canada seem like many countries instead of one. Some Canadians feel more connected to their own regions than to the country as a whole. A fisherman in Newfoundland may have little in common with a cattle rancher from Alberta. The fisherman might see himself as a Newfoundlander and the rancher as an Albertan more than as Canadians. Some people in Quebec even want their province to become a separate country.

At times people's differences and the large distances separating them have created problems. The Canadian government has spent huge sums of money on transportation and communication, trying to draw its people closer together.

In the end, though, Canada is a peaceful and well-to-do country. Most Canadians want all races and all regions in their country to be partners. They believe that this will make for a stronger Canada in the years to come.

A boy enjoys being pulled on a dogsled by a team of huskies on a crisp, clear winter day in Quebec.

3

FAMILY LIFE, FESTIVALS, AND FOOD

Time for Family, Time for Fun

Josh is a fifth-grade student at a public school. He lives in a suburb of Toronto with his parents and older brother. They live in a split-level, three-bedroom home that Josh's parents own. They also own two cars and a boat, which they take on weekend trips to their cottage on Rice Lake, a one-and-a-half-hour drive east from Toronto. Josh himself owns a terrific dog named Hudson.

Josh is a member of a middle-class, English-speaking Canadian family. His family has much in common with other middle-class Canadians. But unlike Josh's parents, who are married, there are many single parents raising children, too. The divorce rate is high—about half of Canadian marriages do not last. Also, many mothers work outside the home—about half of all moms. Both the mother and the father in a family often need to work, to earn enough money to support their family. The average family also has one or two children. Larger families, which used to be the norm in Canada, are becoming less common.

Modern Homes and Mukluks

Many people in Canadian cities live in apartments. Suburban families live in modern houses. Some areas of towns and cities have beautiful old homes, while one-industry, or settlement, towns have quickly-built, simple homes. The houses and streets of small Canadian towns are usually tidy and well kept.

The Inuit of the Arctic no longer live in igloos—dome-shaped homes made out of blocks of hard snow. Instead they live in modern homes with plumbing and central heat. The Inuit have adopted other modern ways too. They are no longer nomads, though many still hunt for food to eat. Most Inuit travel in snowmobiles and cars rather than by dogsled. And they travel by sea in motorboats instead of kayaks. They still sometimes wear their homemade mukluks (MUCK-lucks)—animal-skin boots—or moose-hide parkas and bearskin mitts. But mostly they wear store-bought jeans and sweaters.

Most Inuit today live in tiny, remote towns linked to each other and the rest of Canada only by airplane. They live there because of the good fishing waters or hunting grounds. Some Inuit prefer to live and work in bigger towns. Yellowknife, the capital of the Northwest Territories, is the territory's largest city and boasts modern shopping malls, high-rises, supermarkets, bookstores, suburbs, and fast-food restaurants.

Modern ways have made life easier for Inuit families, no matter where they live in the Arctic, but they have also brought new problems. Television, for example, has for the most part been a destructive force. When Inuit children view television shows, their values and behavior sometimes change. Their new values are different from those of their parents, and this can divide the generations. Many young Inuit people today are drifting away from their age-old family ways.

Inuit children play hockey on the snow near their home at Cape Dorset, Northwest Territories.

Picnics and Pumpkin Pie

No matter where Canadians live, they all enjoy the same national holidays. Children are given a number of days off from school. Canada Day, on July 1, is the country's birthday and is celebrated with picnics and fireworks.

Victoria Day is celebrated at the end of May and honors the birthday of Queen Victoria of Great Britain who lived from

1819 to 1901 and reigned as Britain's queen for sixty-four years. In the province of Quebec the French refuse to honor a British queen, so there this day is called Dollard Day. This holiday honors a French soldier named Dollard des Ormeaux, who lived in the 1600s and is famous for his bravery in battle. He helped seventeen other French Canadians and forty Huron Indians win a battle against three hundred Iroquois. The victory made the fur trade in the region safe against further Iroquois attacks.

Canadians today are also given a day's rest on the Monday following Easter Sunday, on Labor Day in September, on Boxing Day on December 26, on New Year's Day in January, and on Thanksgiving Day. Canadians celebrate Thanksgiving with a stomach-stretching meal of turkey, cranberries, and pumpkin pie. Unlike their neighbors in the United States who enjoy the holiday every November, Canadians celebrate Thanksgiving in October.

Throughout the year, many people across Canada honor their religious holidays, such as Passover celebrated by the Jewish people and Diwali by the Hindus. But the government today gives all Canadians only two religious holidays off from school and work. These are Christmas Day and Good Friday, the Friday before Easter.

Fireworks and Oyster Festivals

Hundreds of festivals are held every year in regions throughout Canada. On June 24, fireworks and bonfires light up Quebec during a festival called *La Fête de la St-Jean-Baptiste*. The province's French people celebrate with parades and parties in honor of the patron saint of Quebec.

In Toronto every summer, the people celebrate with a

Brilliant fireworks over the St. Lawrence River in Montreal, Quebec, celebrate La Fête de la St-Jean-Baptiste.

huge week-long festival called Caribana. This is North America's largest Caribbean festival. Black Canadians make up 1.5 percent of Canada's population, and Caribana is the country's most visible celebration of black heritage. The parade is the highlight of the week, with bands competing for awards. More than five thousand people take part, wearing colorful costumes and riding on floats, dancing to the music of the many bands.

People across Canada also hold festivals to celebrate the seasons. Every February in Quebec City, the people celebrate winter during ten days of parties, winter sports, and parades.

MAPLE SYRUP PIE

The maple tree is so prized in Canada that the tree's leaf is the country's national symbol. Maple syrup has been an important resource to the people for centuries.

In the springtime, when the sap begins to flow in the maple trees, maple syrup festivals are held in many places throughout Canada. Festival workers show how sap is drawn from trees and boiled down to make maple syrup, sugar, and candy. The maple sugar candy is formed into the shape of little maple leaves.

Try making this maple syrup pie, for a delicious slice of Canada! (Be sure to have an adult's help when using a stove, electric mixer, or knife.)

Maple Syrup Pie

2 tablespoons flour
1 tablespoon butter
2 egg yolks
1 cup maple syrup
1/2 cup water

1 9-inch frozen pie shell (buy in the frozen food section at the grocery store)
1 cup whipped cream

This recipe calls for a double boiler. The bottom pot should contain a few inches of water to boil. The top pot will contain the pie mixture.

Bake the frozen pie shell and let cool.

Using an electric mixer, cream the butter and flour together. Ask an adult for help in separating the yolks from the egg whites. Beat the yolks in a small bowl. Add them to the butter and flour and blend well.

Combine the maple syrup and water in another bowl. Add this liquid to the creamed mixture.

Cook in the double boiler until the pie mixture begins to thicken.

Carefully pour into the baked pie crust. Allow the mixture to sit until it hardens.

Cover the pie with a layer of whipped cream and enjoy!

They call their festival the Quebec Winter Carnival. In its snow-bath tradition, people wear bathing suits and run around *barefoot* in the snow! And children love to sail down the giant ice slide that's as high as a three-story building.

Every autumn across Canada, many county fairs honor prized regional foods, such as the Potato Blossom Festival in

New Brunswick or the Oyster Festival in Nova Scotia. And every July, the Calgary Stampede celebrates southern Alberta's Wild West. This world-famous festival is a huge, ten-day-long rodeo. Cowboys come from across Canada and the United States to compete for thousands of dollars in prize money. They put their cowboy skills to the test in about six different rodeo events; among them bareback riding and bull riding. Women compete in the barrel-racing event, riding horses against the clock around three separate barrels and trying not to knock them down.

Many children pull on their cowboy boots and take part in the Stampede, too. In the Mutton-Busting event, five- to eight-year-old cowboys and cowgirls ride sheep, trying to stay on the woolly animals for eight seconds—the standard required time of rodeo events. The children wear hockey hel-

Face painting is one of the fun activities at the annual Blueberry Festival in British Columbia.

Years ago, chuck wagons carried food to cowboys during their long cattle drives. Today the exciting chuck wagon race at the Calgary Stampede tests the speed and skill of wagon drivers.

mets for safety and everyone receives a prize. Cowboys between the ages of ten and fourteen can enter the Junior Steer-Riding Competition.

Broiled Mooseburgers Anyone?

Italy is famous for its pizza and France for its baguettes. Canada does not have one prized national food. Because Canada is a nation of immigrants, people enjoy foods from all over the world.

Green-pea soup is a traditional meal in the province of Quebec. This soup, made from salt pork and dried green peas, was first eaten by the area's early settlers. Many people in Quebec still carry on the tradition today, especially on cold days when warm soup is very welcome.

Ukrainian Canadians eat a popular dish called pierogi (per-OH-gee). Much like ravioli, these dough pockets are filled with mashed potatoes, cheese, onion, or bacon bits and served with sour cream and butter. Children love pierogies as much as adults do.

Canadians in the Atlantic Provinces enjoy everything the sea has to offer. Seafood is prepared in tasty ways, such as lobster salad and golden fried clams.

Much of northern Canada is still wilderness today and plenty of food can be found in Canada's north, such as wild game, game birds, and fish. Clever cooks who live in the Arctic, sub-Arctic, or near the northern lakes and forests take advantage of this. They also find wild berries or wild greens to add to a meal, simply by taking a walk into the woods with a berry bucket.

The main ingredient in some Canadian recipes could only be found in Canada's north. Imagine trying to prepare Barbecued Ribs of Caribou or Broiled Mooseburgers!

One food fact is true for most Canadians, no matter where they live in the country. Their busy lives often lead them to McDonald's and other fast-food restaurants.

Canadian teenage girls looking pleased after a day on the slopes of Bromont ski area in Quebec.

4

SCHOOL AND RECREATION

At School and at Play

"Hi. My name is Jennifer," begins a fifth-grade student from Saskatoon, Saskatchewan, in a letter to her new pen pal in the United States.

"What is school like in Canada?" her American friend has asked. Jennifer enjoys writing letters. She spends more than an hour writing a five-page-long reply!

"I have twenty-seven kids in my classroom," Jennifer tells her new pen pal. "In our school we are not allowed to say swears or throw snowballs or fight or treat other people mean."

Every school has rules. Many Canadian teachers think it is important to teach students about respect and kindness as well as about reading and math.

Jennifer attends a public school in Saskatoon. Canada has both public and private schools for kindergarten through the twelfth grade with many of the private schools run by religious groups. Public schools in Canada are free and open to both girls and boys. Canadian public elementary schools require basic subjects of language, math, social studies, arts, and science.

Canadian students all take French class, too. And at recess

in the wintertime, Jennifer and her classmates ice-skate and play hockey on a rink in the schoolyard. On school field trips, they go downhill and cross-country skiing. In the Arctic recess must be held indoors some days—because of polar bears! When polar bears aren't roaming around, children play out-side, even when temperatures drop to -20ºF (-29ºC).

Jennifer likes school and most of her classmates do too. But there are some children in Canada who do not always benefit from Canada's public school system. These include Indian and Inuit children. Years ago the only public education available to many of the country's native children was taught by white teachers and based in white culture. This was not successful in educating native children. Many Indian and Inuit teenagers dropped out of school, and without an educa-tion they couldn't find good jobs.

About twenty years ago some Indian and Inuit communi-ties began to educate their own children in their own way. They taught classes in their native languages, based lessons on their folktales and arts and crafts, and sometimes organized the school year so that pupils would have time to hunt and fish with their families. Educated this way, Indian and Inuit chil-dren get better grades and fewer teenagers drop out of school. Yet even more must be done today to help native children and teenagers experience success in school—as much success as Jennifer enjoys in Saskatoon.

On Holiday

All Canadians take some time away from school and from work for vacations. Many travel to one of the country's thirty-four wilderness areas in national parks. Others travel to lake-side cottages where they water-ski or canoe.

Canadian Navajo and Hopi Indian teenagers learn new skills in their community high school's computer class.

Many Canadians take day trips to museums. The Royal Tyrrell Museum of Palaeontology, in the badlands of Alberta near Drumheller, contains the world's largest display of complete dinosaur skeletons. In the summer, visitors can take part in digs in the dinosaur quarries.

Canadians also find many ways to have fun in the wintertime. The snow draws many people outdoors to sled and ski. Canadians love to skate on the thousands of ice-covered lakes, too.

Taking trips south to warmer climates in the wintertime is also very popular. Many Canadians choose warm places filled with sunshine to visit, such as Florida or California in the United States. This is a sure way to escape Canada's cold winters.

41

Sports in the North

Millions of Canadians love watching sports on television and at stadiums or playing the game themselves. Canada's most popular sport is hockey. This game began in Canada in the 1850s when British soldiers played a form of their country's field hockey game. In the 1870s Canadian students drew up the first formal ice hockey rules at McGill University in Montreal. Canadians today love watching the professional teams and practicing their own moves in their hometown rinks. There are hockey leagues for men, women, and children.

The National Hockey League (NHL) has twenty-six

Pickup hockey games are popular among many Canadian kids. These teenagers are playing boot hockey on a snow-covered road.

North American teams. Seven are based in Canada. Although many NHL teams are located in the United States, most of the league players are Canadian. The NHL season lasts from October to April, followed by the Stanley Cup playoffs among the top teams from April to June. The winning team receives the Stanley Cup, the highest professional honor in North American hockey.

Winter games provide most of Canada's sports heroes, and for years, star hockey players especially have been treated as national heroes. Canada has produced hundreds of great hockey players in the twentieth century including Mario Lemieux, Patrick Roy, and Wayne Gretzky.

Canadian superstar hockey player, Wayne Gretzky from Ontario, played for the Edmonton Oilers between 1978 and 1988. Today he plays for the Los Angeles Kings. In 1993 Gretzky was the NHL's highest-paid player, earning eleven million dollars that year. He is known as "The Great One," and many people consider him to be the best hockey player who ever lived.

Canada is also famous for its figure skaters, speed skaters, and skiers. Two recent stars are Elvis Stojko of Ontario and Myriam Bédard of Quebec. Stojko was the world champion in men's figure

Wayne Gretzky of the Los Angeles Kings celebrates after making his historic 802nd career goal, which broke the all-time NHL scoring record.

43

OLYMPIC DREAMS

Myriam Bédard won her twin gold medals at the Winter Olympics by remaining true to a dream. Ever since she was a young girl, Myriam dreamed that one day she would compete at the Olympic Games.

Myriam Bédard waves to the crowd after winning a gold medal in the 1994 Olympic biathlon.

Myriam Bédard (pronounced bay-DAR) was born and raised in Neufchâtel, Quebec. During the 1970s, when she was eight, Myriam saw a film at school about the Olympics and imagined herself winning a medal in figure skating. Myriam took skating lessons and entered competitions, but by the time she was twelve she decided skating wouldn't get her to the Olympics. She knew she had the necessary strength but not the artistic response to music that's needed to win.

What sport would take Myriam to the Olympics? She discovered it at age fifteen. The teenager spent weekends as an army cadet at a military base in Quebec. Myriam learned to shoot at the base, and since she had also skied several times, she decided to race in the base's Winter Games biathlon event one weekend. It didn't matter that she wore borrowed ski boots that were too big— she won the race.

Myriam soon began to race in national biathlon competitions and came out on top. In 1991 she started to win World Cup events and rapidly climbed the ladder to the Olympics.

In 1992 she won a bronze medal at the Olympic Games in Albertville, France. In 1994 she won two gold medals at the Winter Olympics in Lillehammer, Norway—in spite of wearing mismatched skis, an error she discovered after the race!

Myriam Bédard is a strong and talented athlete. She combined her ability with a determination to turn her childhood fantasy into reality—and made her Olympic dreams come true. In 1995 Myriam was inducted into the Canadian Sports Hall of Fame.

skating in 1995. Bédard was the first Canadian woman ever to win two gold medals at a Winter Olympics. In 1994 she received her two golds for the biathlon, a sport that combines cross-country skiing and rifle shooting.

Curling is another popular Canadian winter sport that comes from Scotland. One player on a team pushes a large, round stone across an icy surface toward a target. The other team players sweep brooms on the ice in front of the stone. The sweeping helps guide the stone toward the target.

Winter sports help Canadians in the Arctic pass their long cold season. Every two years, a different town in Canada's far north hosts the Arctic Winter Games. Athletes from all over the Arctic—including Russia and Greenland—compete in these games. All of the sports events are northern in nature, such as skiing, hockey, dogsledding, and snowshoeing. The events also include traditional Inuit and Dene Indian games. Thousands of years ago, the Dene settled in Canada's subarctic regions, and most of their tribe today lives in Yellowknife, the Northwest Territories.

A downhill skier defies gravity on a beautiful slope in the Canadian Rockies.

One Inuit sport played at the Arctic Winter Games is "the airplane." The athlete lies on the floor facedown with his legs together and arms spread out. The player has three assistants. One assistant holds the athlete's feet tightly. The other two assistants hold tightly on to his arms. The assistants lift the athlete off the

45

floor. His strength is tested as he tries to remain stiff as a board as long as possible. The athlete who lasts the longest before buckling wins the medal.

Arctic Canadians also host summer sporting events. The Midnight Golf Tournament is held each year in Yellowknife late in June—the time in the Arctic year when the sun never sets. Playing golf at midnight in the Arctic is one fun way of celebrating summer.

Ice-skating is one of the most popular cold-weather sports among Canadians.

Throughout Canada, hockey has always been the favorite sport, but other games are growing in popularity. While only a few Canadians play professional baseball, major league teams—the Montreal Expos and the Toronto Blue Jays— attract millions of fans. The Blue Jays stadium, the Toronto Sky-dome, is thirty-one stories tall. It is the world's largest stadium and has the world's first roof to completely open and close.

Football is a popular Canadian sport, too. The Canadian Football League (CFL) has eight professional teams based in cities across Canada as well as five from the United States. There are a few small differences between Canadian and American football. The Canadian field is longer and wider, so Canadian football is more of a passing game. There are twelve players on a Canadian team instead of the eleven on an American one, and there are only three downs instead of four.

Canadians have never paid much attention to basketball. It's a winter sport and competes with hockey for fans and players. But the National Basketball Association established Canadian teams in Vancouver and Toronto, which began play in the 1995–1996 season. The sport may become popular in Canada, as baseball has in recent years.

Canadian children across the country play sports of all sorts such as volleyball, basketball, soccer, and football. Hockey leagues are very popular. Canadian children may compete in leagues starting at age seven, and both boys and girls may play in the leagues.

On Christmas Eve and Christmas morning across the country, hundreds of children eagerly open presents containing new hockey equipment. They tug on their new helmets, shin pads, and jerseys and can hardly wait for Christmas dinner to be over so they can get to the skating rink.

Many Canadian children who play hockey dream of joining the National Hockey League some day. Their parents encourage this competition. They make great sacrifices of time and money to see that their children get the most ice time. The love of hockey has brought millions of Canadians closer together in spirit.

Canadian artist Alphonse Pare carved this very large mural out of pinewood and painted it with watercolors.

5

THE ARTS

Stars of the North

One Saturday morning a ten-year-old Canadian boy tugs on a pair of jeans. A U.S. company probably designed them. For breakfast the boy munches on a bowl of sugar-coated cereal made by a U.S. food company. After breakfast the boy watches a television show produced in the United States, then reads a book by an American writer published in the United States.

Throughout the twentieth century, the United States has had a large influence on Canada's culture. Many of the popular fashions, foods, fads, songs, books, and magazines enjoyed by Canadians come from the United States.

Some Canadians are concerned by the tremendous impact the United States has had on their lives. They feel overpowered by the superpower to the south. The Canadian government agrees that the United States has molded the lives of Canadians too much. The government is also unhappy when many of Canada's best artists, actors, and musicians choose to live and work in the United States, lured by the promise of wealth and fame.

During the past twenty-five years, the Canadian government has worked hard to change this pattern and make Canada's own culture stronger. The government has given grants to many Canadian artists to help them become successful at home. It has supported Canadian authors and artists who want to create television shows, movies, music, and theater and dance productions.

The government also began a new policy: 80 percent of Canadian television broadcasts have to be produced by Canadians. This cut back on the number of U.S.-produced television shows and movies shown in Canada. The Canadian Broadcasting Corporation (CBC) supports more Canadian artists by airing their music, drama, poetry, and films.

Thirty percent of music played on radio stations has to be written or performed by Canadians, too. This new policy has caused a music boom in Canada with many talented singers and songwriters becoming successful.

The Canadian government's efforts in the arts have paid off during the past twenty-five years. Canada has a lively, rich culture today. Toronto, Ontario, is known as the arts showcase of English-speaking Canada. Toronto has Canada's largest number of art galleries, theaters, and concert halls. Most Canadian books are published in Toronto. And most Canadian movies are filmed there, too.

Totem Poles and Soapstone Seals

Even without the help of the Canadian government, native painters, carvers, musicians, and designers have created beautiful art for centuries. Before Europeans set foot on Canada's shores in the 1500s, this northern land had many wonderful artists. Most Indian tribes were carvers, and the Haida (HI-dah)

Eaton Centre is the largest shopping center in Toronto, Ontario. It contains several galleries and shops that sell art created by Inuit carvers and other Canadian artists.

of the Pacific Coast were some of the best. They carved detailed masks and totem poles that told the stories of their ancestors.

The Inuit in Canada's far north have been carvers for centuries, too. Through the years they have used their age-old skills to carve animal and human figures out of ivory, bone, and soapstone. Today Inuit carvings are shown in galleries

A close-up of one section of a tall totem pole, which was carved by Haida Indians years ago and still stands in British Columbia today.

across Canada and are famous the world over. Art collectors from around the world buy Inuit carvings for high prices.

Carving is one of the Inuit people's chief ways of earning a living today. Stone dust can be dangerous if breathed into the lungs, so many Inuit sculptors work outdoors, even in the wintertime. Before beginning a new sculpture, an Inuit carver often stares at the rock for a long time, trying to sense the spirit of the animal or person inside. Only then does the artist start to carve. Soon the animal or human figure that was hidden inside the rock begins to appear.

Modern Canada has produced many painters too. The nation's most famous artists lived in the 1920s and were known as The Group of Seven. These seven artists—among them J. E. H. MacDonald and A. Y. Jackson—painted scenes of Canada's beautiful wilderness in a similar style, using bold strokes and bright colors.

Northern Storytellers

Canada has also produced many skilled storytellers and writers through the years. Inuit legends have been passed down by word of mouth for centuries. Some of the most famous of these are about Sedna, the sea goddess. According to Inuit legend, Sedna controls all the sea and is half-woman and half-fish.

Many famous writers and books have also come out of Canada. In the late 1800s Lucy Maud Montgomery was born and raised in Prince Edward Island. In the early 1900s she wrote her famous *Anne of Green Gables* series. The books feature a lively, red-haired orphan girl named Anne. Much like Anne who was raised by adoptive parents, Maud (the name the author chose for herself over Lucy) was raised by her grandparents and had a lonely childhood. Maud's mother died before Maud's second birthday. Maud's father was absent during most of her childhood. In spite of her loneliness as a child, Maud let nothing stand in the way of her becoming a writer. Although she died in 1942, Maud is Canada's best-selling woman writer today, and her books are read around the world.

Farley Mowat is another well-known Canadian author of much-loved children's books. Born in Ontario, Farley has written a number of classics such as *The Dog Who Wouldn't Be* and *Owls in the Family*. His book *Never Cry Wolf* was made into a Walt Disney movie. Farley has sold more books than any other Canadian writer—ten million copies in fifty countries and translated into twenty-two languages.

Gordon Korman, who was born in Montreal and lives in

The Whale Hunt, *a print by Canadian artist Mary Pudlap, shows how the Inuit used to hunt in their kayaks years ago.*

Ontario today, is the author of many funny children's books. Among his popular books are *The Son of Interflux* and the Bugs Potter series. Gordon wrote his first book, *This Can't Be Happening at Macdonald Hall!*, when he was twelve years old. He got carried away writing a seventh-grade English assignment and wrote a 120-page-long story—a whole book! He decided to try to publish it and succeeded. His novel was published two years later by Scholastic Publishing Company in New York. Since then Gordon has written another book every summer, to the delight of his many fans across North America.

Stars of Stage and Screen

Canada has also produced hundreds of television and movie stars and dozens of famous comedians. Jim Carrey, born and raised in Ontario, is an extremely funny comedian and one of Hollywood's most in-demand actors today. Jim played the lead roles in *Ace Ventura: Pet Detective, Ace Ventura: When Nature Calls, The Mask,* and *Dumb and Dumber.* In the mid-1990s, Jim was paid ten million dollars to play the part of the Riddler in *Batman Forever.*

THE BALLAD OF THE NORTHERN LIGHTS

Robert Service, who lived between 1874 and 1958, is Canada's best-known poet. He was born in England, spent his childhood years in Scotland, and then emigrated to Canada. He wrote many poems and ballads about Canada's northern wilderness and the gold rush of 1898, including one called "The Ballad of the Northern Lights." Northern lights are bands of bright light and color that appear in the northern sky at night, especially in the Arctic. The following is the final stanza from this ballad.

Some say that the Northern Lights are the glare of the Arctic ice and
    snow;
And some that it's electricity, and nobody seems to know.
But I'll tell you now—and if I lie, may my lips be stricken dumb—
It's a mine, a mine of the precious stuff that men call radium.
It's a million dollars a pound, they say, and there's tons and tons in
    sight.
You can see it gleam in a golden stream in the solitudes of night.
And it's mine, all mine—and say! if you have a hundred plunks
    [bucks] to spare,
I'll let you have the chance of your life, I'll sell you a quarter share.
You turn it down? Well, I'll make it ten seeing as you are my friend.
Nothing doing? Say! don't be hard—have you got a dollar to lend?
Just a dollar to help me out, I know you'll treat me white [fairly];
I'll do as much for you some day. . . . God bless you, sir; good-night.

A breathtaking moment during a performance of Montreal's Cirque du Soleil.

Michael J. Fox is a Canadian actor who stars in both comedy and drama. Born in Edmonton, Alberta, Michael played the part of Alex on the television series *Family Ties* in the 1980s. He also played the lead role in the popular *Back to the Future* movies.

Thousands of talented Canadian actors perform in theaters across the country today. The colorful and fanciful Cirque du Soleil, meaning "Circus of the Sun," is based in Montreal. This French-Canadian show blends theater and circus. It uses no animals—all of its performers are people. A special school trains children and adults to work for this theater as acrobats, trapeze artists, actors, and dancers.

Three great Canadian ballet companies perform regularly around the world to packed houses. These are the Royal Winnipeg Ballet, Les Grands Ballets Canadiens of Montreal, and Toronto's National Ballet of Canada.

Canada also has many fine musicians. Neil Young has been popular among rock fans for decades. Raffi writes and sings songs for young children. Oscar Peterson is a legendary jazz piano player. k. d. lang's success spans pop and country music, with her albums selling by the millions. As a child, k. d. always admired Canadian musicians and felt proud when a Canadian became a success. Today there are hundreds of Canadians she may feel proud of, including herself!

This Great Land

Why is Canada a great land? It is a well-to-do nation, where most citizens enjoy a good quality of life. It offers plenty of space to its people, and each region has sights that fill people's hearts with awe.

In 1990 the United Nations voted Canada the Number One country. Canada earned its first-place score because of the amount of money people earn, how educated the people are, and how long Canadians can expect to live.

Canadians have many reasons to appreciate their nation. And most people do. They feel fortunate to live in this vast land that stretches from sea to sea to sea.

Country Facts

Official Name: Canada

Capital: Ottawa

Location: in North America; bordered on the south and northwest by the United States; on the west by the Pacific Ocean, on the east by the Atlantic Ocean, and by the Arctic Ocean to the north

Area: approximately 3,850,000 square miles (9,971,500 square kilometers). *Greatest distances*: east–west, 3,400 miles (5,471 kilometers); north–south, 2,730 miles (4,393 kilometers)

Elevation: *Highest*: Mount Logan in the Yukon Territory, 19,850 feet (6,050 meters) above sea level. *Lowest*: sea level along the coast

Climate: Highly varied, from moderate to bitterly cold Arctic. In the southern areas, summers are mild and winters are long and cold.

Population: approximately 29 million. *Distribution*: about 20 percent rural, 80 percent urban

Form of Government: Parliamentary democracy. The government is modeled after that of the United States and Britain, with a legislative branch, consisting of a Senate and a House of Commons.

Important Products: *Agriculture*: wheat, barley, fruit, vegetables, milk, meat. *Industries*: motor vehicle production, pulp and paper manufacturing, iron and steel milling, machinery and equipment manufacturing, mining, extraction of mineral fuels, fishing, forestry. *Natural Resources*: natural gas, crude oil, coal, gold, iron ore, silver, molybdenum, uranium, zinc, forests, water

Basic Unit of Money: Canadian dollar; 1 Canadian dollar = 100 cents

Languages: English and French are the official national languages.

Religion: Christianity is the major religion. Roman Catholics (45 percent), Protestants (36 percent); non-Christian religions include Judaism, Islam, Hinduism, Sikhism, and Buddhism.

Flag: red maple leaf on a white square, with a red bar (one-half the width of the square) on each side of the white field

National Anthem: *O Canada*

Major Holidays: New Year's Day; Good Friday, Friday before Easter; Easter; Easter Monday, the Monday after Easter; Victoria Day, fourth Monday in May; Canada Day, July 1; Labor Day, first Monday in September; Thanksgiving Day, second Monday in October; Christmas Day; Boxing Day, December 26

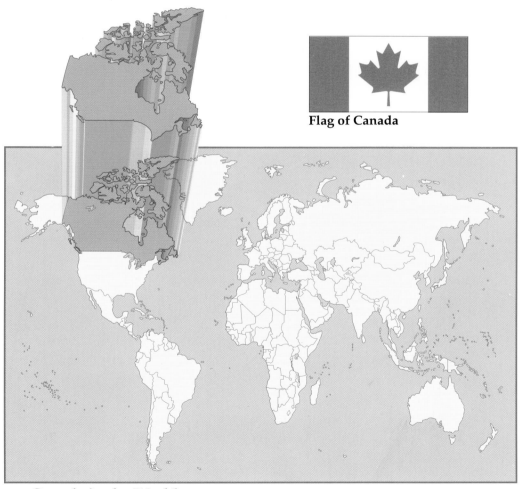

Flag of Canada

Canada in the World

59

Glossary

Arctic: polar region of the earth that lies north of the treeline; point where the weather becomes too cold for trees to grow

badlands: dry, desertlike region where few plants are able to grow

bilingual: able to speak one's native language and another equally well. In Canada this usually means English and French.

curling: Scottish winter sport in which players push large stones across an icy surface toward a target

hoodoo: natural pillar left standing when sandy rock around it is eroded away by the forces of wind and water

igloo: dome-shaped house made out of blocks of hard snow

Inuit (IN-oo-it, IN-yoo-it)**:** native people who settled in Arctic regions

Métis (may-TEE) **Indian:** person who is part Indian and part French

Mountie: nickname for a member of Canada's national police force, the Royal Canadian Mounted Police

mukluk (MUCK-luck)**:** soft boot worn by the Inuit, often lined with fur and made of sealskin or reindeer skin

northern lights: also called the aurora borealis (uh-RHOR-uh bohr-ee-AL-uhs); bands of bright light and color that appear in the northern sky at night, especially in the Arctic

Nunavut (NUN-uh-vuht)**:** a new territory in Canada to be governed by the Inuit people; *nunavut* means "our land" in the Inuit language

permafrost: ground that remains frozen year-round

pierogi (per-OH-gee)**:** dough pocket filled with potatoes, cheese, onion, or sauerkraut

prime minister: top leader in countries with a parliament

province: geographic division in certain countries, similar to a state in the United States

subarctic: area immediately surrounding the Arctic Circle

tundra: vast, treeless plains of the Arctic regions

voyageur (voi-uh-ZHAR)**:** young man hired to search North America's wilderness for fur-trading native people; also hired to act as a woodsman, boatsman, and guide and to transport supplies

For Further Reading

Andronik, Catherine M. *Kindred Spirit*. New York: Atheneum, 1993. (A biography of L. M. Montgomery.)

Cheng, Pang Guek. *Canada*. Cultures of the World. New York: Marshall Cavendish, 1994.

Flint, David. *Canada*. On the Map. Austin, Texas: Raintree Steck-Vaughn, 1993.

Harrison, Ted. *O Canada*. New York: Ticknor & Fields, 1993.

Kalman, Bobbie. *Canada Celebrates Multiculturalism*. New York: Crabtree, 1993.

Kalman, Bobbie. *Canada: The Culture*. New York: Crabtree, 1993.

Korman, Gordon. *Radio Fifth Grade*. New York: Scholastic, 1989.

Lotz, Jim. *Nova Scotia*. Discover Canada. (Other titles are available about other provinces.) Toronto: Grolier Limited, 1991.

Malcolm, Andrew H. *The Land and People of Canada*. New York: HarperCollins, 1991.

Montgomery, L. M. *Anne of Green Gables*. New York: Bantam, 1987.

Mowat, Farley. *Owls in the Family*. New York: Bantam, 1985.

Shepherd, Jenifer. *Canada*. Enchantment of the World. Chicago: Childrens Press, 1987.

Index

Page numbers for illustrations are in boldface

About the Author

During her sixth- through ninth-grade school years, Shelley Swanson Sateren lived in the Canadian provinces of Alberta and Saskatchewan. She spent many weekends and summer days on vacation with her family and friends in the Canadian Rocky Mountains, in the Alberta badlands, and at her family's cabin in northern Alberta. In high school Sateren returned to Alberta, where she spent a summer working as a counselor at a children's camp.

Sateren has since worked as a children's book editor and as a clerk in a children's bookstore. She is also a certified elementary schoolteacher. Sateren has written stories and articles for magazines and four books for children—one of them about Banff National Park in the Canadian Rockies. She lives in St. Paul, Minnesota, with her husband and young son.